Praises to My King

Christmas Messages
from the Heart

"Babe in the Manger"

Drawing contributed by Nevaeh Hull.

Natalie Selena Bee

Scripture quotations marked NKJV are taken from the New King James Version of the Bible.

Scripture quotations marked KJV are taken from the King James Version of the Bible.

Scripture quotations marked MSG are taken from The Message Version of the Bible.

Scripture quotations marked TLB are taken from The Living Bible Version of the Bible.

Scripture quotations marked NIV are taken from the New International Version of the Bible.

Dedication

"Praises to My King: Christmas Messages from the Heart" is dedicated to the loving memory of my Mom, Minnie Ophelia Washington Bee. Throughout the years she would be one of the first people to hear my finished work. She would use my poems as her Christmas card for years. She would encourage me, not only with my writings, but in everything I do.

As an educator, my Mom made sure her children received a good education. She knew that I could write creatively. I can remember her teaching me to read and write as a little girl. Mommy knew I would succeed if I was persistent. Whether it was the classroom, Sunday school or Bible study, I learned. My Mom transitioned to be with the Lord four years ago. I miss the moments of sharing with her. I still feel she is with me, especially when I am writing.

To my cheerleader, Mommy, I dedicate this book to you.

Acknowledgements

Throughout the years of writing poetry, it has truly been a real journey. Having the opportunity to share my heart and the hearts of others is a blessing. I thank God for ordering my steps on this journey. It means the world to me. This ministry He has blessed me with, blesses so many people. It is your blessings that keep me going. It is the gift of life, God, that You breathe into me every day. I acknowledge You, God, as the head of my life. Thank you for the defining moments in my life I continue to experience.

Thank you to my pastor, Dr. Carl Morris. He is always a supporter and guiding force in the endeavors God has placed in me. I appreciate your words of encouragement and all the prayers. Thank you to my Abundant Life Church family. I'm so grateful to be a part of this ministry.

Thank you to my family and friends, other supporters of my writings. Thank you for the encouragement and reminding me to be open to the possibilities.

Introduction

For many years, I have written a Christmas poem to share with others. The message is about the birth of Jesus Christ. It is important to tell what His life represents. Part of writing poetry, gives me the freedom to express my thoughts, emotions, and heart. That is the message I wanted to share. The word of faith has fashioned me to be the person God has called me to be. As I write, I give Him all the praises. This is my ministry.

I want to share some comments from a few of my family and friends. They are the ones who have received my Christmas messages over the years:

"Natalie, you have blessed me, our family, and the world with your beautiful heart inspired poetic writings of what our Savior Jesus Christ means to you and so many of us. Your words are spirit-inspired, touch our hearts and always give glory to God. In our home, your Christmas poems have been read aloud, then posted on our door or Christmas tree. Thank you!" L.W.

"I am always so encouraged by the Christmas poems I receive from my sister in Christ. They help me to value my family and friends as we approach the celebration of our Lord's birth. They often point out the true meaning of the birth of our Lord Jesus Christ. They help me to embrace the love of our Lord in a time that sometimes are a bit painful because we are missing love ones that have transitioned on with the Lord. They point out the true joy we should have as we commemorate our Savior's birth. Most of all they remind me of His unchanging sacrificial love for me which I should cherish and share with others. I am so grateful for the light hearted encouraging truth revealing the message of Christmas my Lord and Savior's birth when I receive my poem each year." B.J.

"My family and I eagerly await Natalie's Christmas poems each year. Her poems not only put us in the Christmas spirit, but they remind us about the true reason we celebrate Christmas; the birth of our Lord and Savior Jesus Christ." C.M.

It is always a pleasure to be an honor recipient of Natalie Bee's poem each year as well as on other occasions. Her poems provide an opportunity for those, privilege to receive, to see how God wants her to share her love for Him to others. One can see hope, encouragement and always a defining point of focus on mankind. B.E.B.

"The beautiful artistry of Natalie Bee's poetry brings an inspiring, impactful and powerful message full of warmth and wisdom to the reader. The Spirit of the Lord has given Natalie beautiful words that has truly set the ambiance for me and my family in this holiday season. She gives a gift to all of the wonderful treasures our Heavenly Father wants to bestow upon us. Natalie's exceptional talent and skills, truly pulls me into the realm where God resides. Thank you, Natalie, for your wisdom, love and commitment in hearing the voice of the Lord and writing His love to us in poetry." L.M.J.

"Natalie Bee's poems are inspiring and uplifting. They also give one of a great sense of peace and still the soul. I find them to give me a great sense of pleasure in both positive moments and during stressful times. Every time I read one they give me a new thought or insight. I always look forward to seeing more from her." M.L.M.

"The holidays are absolutely my most favorite time of the year. The remembrance of Jesus' birth, the moments shared with family, and Natalie's beautiful poetry. Often times the commercial aspect of the season can overshadow the true meaning of the holiday. Natalie's Christmas poems are always a timely reminder of the true meaning of the season. Her poetry is intentional and impactful. Her writing speaks of love and hope, and the poems never fail to inspire me." K.G.

"I feel that the poems are very uplifting and inspiring. They are a breath of fresh air. The poems are a way of reminding you of what the season is all about: love, giving, faith, and belief in the awesome God we serve. These poems are very calming and spiritual and definitely are a blessing to me and my family!!! We look forward to receiving them every year." S. W.

"Thank you, Natalie Bee, for all of the inspirational poems over the years. You are truly a follower of the Most High God in the Name of Jesus and the Holy Spirit." D. M.

"Each year I look forward to receiving Natalie Bee's books of Poetic Inspiration and Expressions as well as her Christmas poems. The poems explore many aspects of life's issues. They allow a person to understand where they have been in their life and how they move on successfully in the future. Additionally, the poems provide a wealth of food for thought for Devotions and Bible Study. I am looking forward to what the latest book will offer." R.A.

"Natalie is a gifted writer. I have been receiving her Christmas writings since 1999. It is truly a gift that I look forward to opening each Christmas. Natalie's Christmas writings always convey the message of love and serves to remind its' readers of the real meaning of Christmas and who it is that we should all celebrate. In these times when so much of the focus of such a significant event is commercialized. I am grateful, thankful and blessed to be reminded that it is the birth of JESUS CHRIST that we celebrate. And to that I say...Happy Birthday JESUS!" CP

"Natalie demonstrates her love of family by assisting in organizing 30 years of family reunions, tireless genealogy work and strong family ties. Each year we know that the holiday is fast approaching when we receive one of her festive poems. Her collection of poems over the years give us a strong sense of family, faith, and love. The poems are nostalgic, inspiring, soothing and reflective pieces of work. I look forward to receiving one each year. I'm very excited about her new Christmas project which will be shared with the world. God Bless you in all of your endeavors." SA

Table of Contents

An Event for Everyone

---

⁹ Suddenly an angel appeared among them, and the landscape shone bright with the glory of the Lord. They were badly frightened, ¹⁰ but the angel reassured them.

"Don't be afraid!" he said. "I bring you the most joyful news ever announced, and it is for everyone! ¹¹ The Savior—yes, the Messiah, the Lord—has been born tonight in Bethlehem![b] ¹² How will you recognize him? You will find a baby wrapped in a blanket,[c] lying in a manger!"

---

¹³ Suddenly, the angel was joined by a vast host of others—the armies of heaven—praising God.

Luke 2:9-13 (TLB)

A Christmas Season of Love

A Christmas season of love --
filled with joy and peace.
A time of giving.
A time to release.

Family and friends
they are so important to me.
United together in love,
success, and victory.

God our Father.
Jesus, His awesome Son.
Lead us this Christmas season
as new life has begun.

Joy and all the hope that it brings.
Peace and happiness.
Hear the bells ring.
Joy to the world…the carolers sing.

Frost on our noses.
Chills on our toes.
Warmth in our hearts.
Many smiles that shine and glow.

Happy I am, as the year ends.
It has been great.
A combination of time spent with
wonderful family and friends.

Celebrate the love Jesus has for you.
Take a moment for a heartfelt, "Thank you!"
I wish you much happiness as the year ends.
Have a blessed tomorrow as a new year begins.

A Heart Filled with Love

A heart filled with love is what you require of me.
A special feeling that comes from deep within.
Oh, Jesus this is the season for love and compassion to be shown.
For You set the example so long ago.

On Christmas Day, You, the Son of God was born.
A unique and priceless gift of love.
Jesus Your life was divinely given.
A treasure to walk through life and share with others.

Thank you, God, for loving us so.
You gave Your best an awesome Savior and Redeemer.
It is He who calls us friend.
As we gather with family and friends, a heart filled with love flows.
Thank you, Jesus Christ, for You are the one we love and adore.
The Anointed One who reigns.

As I look around, I can truly see.
Every blessing that is before me.
So, I say "Hallelujah" to the lamb.
"Hallelujah" for the One that You are.
Abba provided You the One to set the captive free.
Oh, Lord Jesus how You love me.

I pray the season won't depart.
Without you capturing someone else's heart.
May they come to know the true meaning of Christmas.
Jesus that is You – a heart filled with love.

This Christmas season filled with splendor and grace.
My sweet Jesus, I wait for the day when we are face to face.
Until then, I share You with all that I know.

No man could write this script.
It is so much more than that.
It is a heart filled with love and that is a fact.
I pray the joy of Christmas will bless all who embrace it today.

"For to us a child is born…" (Isaiah 9:6 NIV)

A Season Just For You

The year is about to end.
What have you done my friend?
The beauty of life has flown through our hands.
Some days are easy, some with heavy demands.

But through it all, something remains the same.
That is the love of our Savior, our Lord, and our King.
Divine in spirit, in knowledge, and in truth.
Destiny abounds throughout me and you.

A gift one should receive so willingly.
No price tag attached or cost to defray.
Just accept the love of Jesus, as it comes your way.

The season is special,
for all who know
the love of the Father as He shows.

During this holiday season, share the love of Jesus.
Enjoy the splendor that He has to offer.
Not only to me,
but also everyone that you see.

Spread the joy, the love, and the peace of God.
Not just during the holiday season,
but as each day comes and goes.
You know Him and His love, so...
this is a season just for you.

"for unto us a child is born." Isaiah 9:6 NKJV)

A Season of Gratitude and Praise

A season of gratitude and praise my heart sings to me.
So much I've been blessed with and
how much my Heavenly Father means.
When I think of the goodness of the Lord,
oh the many praises that resonate within my spirit.
I want to shout it loud from the mountain tops.

The many daily blessings from God
not for granted do I take them you see.
They flow from Him, to you and to me.
Blessed and highly favored this season of gratitude is.
The praises flow from my mouth and deep within.
As I rejoice over my Savior, my Confidant, and my Friend.

This relationship is personal, bountiful, intimate, and true.
Thank you, Jesus, thank you.
I open my eyes each day and my heart is beating too.
All I can say is "Hallelujah" Lord - my soul blesses you.

When I look around and see all Thou have created, I'm blessed.
Amazed I am Lord of all Your wondrous works.
This blessed Savior was born for me.
Over two thousand years ago God knew
His perfect plan would come to be.
His people needed redemption; the captive set free.

Words of blessing freely they flow.
Words of thankfulness are released.
With words of gratitude and praise Heavenly places are found.
My prayers I ask and Your blessings are given.
The Presence of the Lord - as I seek His face - I do find.
The doors of opportunity as I knock are opened wide.

These words of gratitude and praise continuously do I offer.
They make me who I am in You Lord every day.
This season of gratitude draws me closer to You.
I will continue to live, trust, surrender, and praise You.
Words of gratitude I lift to Jesus my Precious Savior.
Especially during this sacred day,
You get all the glory and the praise.

"I will bless the Lord at all times; His praise shall continually
be in my mouth." Psalm 34:1 (KJV)

And the greatest of these...LOVE

Love, a four-lettered word,
  not to be taken lightly.
It has made the hearts of man
  survive, exist, desire, and succeed.

When I think of love,
It leads me to family, friends, and Christ.
In family, one can share good times and bad.
With friends, you can also be happy and sad.
With Christ, His love is unconditional and true!

Remember to always tell those
  important to you that you love them.
Tomorrow is never promised to anyone.
Opportunities are given, don't let them pass away.

My love is great for you all.
Knowing you are there whenever I call.
The unitedness of a family with a bond so strong.
One never feels like they don't belong.

Special, rare, and full of truth.
I express my love to all of you.
This season, this holiday, this time of peace.
May the love of Christ never cease.

"And now abide faith, hope, love, these three; but the greatest of these is love." I Corinthians 13:13 (NKJV)

Celebrate This Season

The holiday season fastly approaching.
The aroma of many different things in the air.
The sweet smells that come from the kitchen.
The smell of pine, fir, and cedar too.
The Christmas trees fresh & new.

The cool breezes as they pass your face,
But do you really know it is His grace!
This holiday season sit back and reflect.
What does it really mean to me?
A bunch of gifts? Someone born for you and me?
A birth that happened to set us free?

Join me in celebrating this Christmas day.
For Christ was born to show us the way!
Experience the life of joy, peace, and happiness.
The Father gave the best gift of all.
His Son's birth and His death!

No one exempt unless they choose.
No one denied unless they refuse.
No one on earth could give a greater gift.
The birth of our Savior.

Thank you, Father, for a gift so free.
Not only for me, but for you and you!
Celebrate the season and the joy that it brings,
As your heart rejoices in the songs you sing.
Let's Celebrate Jesus --- you & me!

God's Love: Taking a Stand for the King

All hail King Jesus every man.
His birth is echoed all across the land.
Our blessed Savior Jesus is He.
You came in wonder, love, and majesty.

He reigns, He reigns, the people sing.
Blessed we are because He reigns.
Glorify Him, the Wonderful Counselor is He.
Jesus You reign in love, power, and peace.

Our Heavenly Father sent His only Son.
Yes, for each and every one.
Faith, hope, joy, and the magnificence He brings.
As we say "Hallelujah" to the newborn King.
In God's love our voices ring.
Taking a stand for the King.

Such a precious life that is born on Christmas Day.
An effective message that is truly needed as we pray.
It conquers the hatred and bitterness that surrounds us.
It stifles discrimination, jealousy, and evil tendencies too.
Jesus's love is stronger than any of you.
Read God's Word and you will see.

King Jesus you experienced this life too.
You stood strong as you proclaimed love is what we should do.
So no weapon formed against me shall prosper.
Yes, I'll pray for my enemies more than ever today.

The Bible says, "…have fervent love for one another."
An ambassador of Christ I will be toward all in God's family.
Love restored; life restored; total restoration is our victory.
Love is exclaimed throughout the land.
As I join King Jesus and take a stand.

Thank you, Jesus, we adore You.
We must continue to pray for our fellow man too.
We will be able to proclaim, "Mission Accomplished".
This is in Jesus Name!
As I take a stand for the King.

Isaiah 54:17; Galatians 5:22-23; Matthew 5:43; I Peter 4:8

I Love You: A Christmas Message

The Christmas season is already here.
Upon my face I feel the refreshing brisk air.
Scurrying around so many people I see.
From this store to that store in search of the perfect gift.

The perfect and precious gift I seek is priceless.
There is no financial value at all.
It is worth more than all the silver and gold.
This gift has three words attached to it.
 "I love you." It can be the hardest thing to say.
Words our Heavenly Father demonstrates in His own way.
It came in a package uniquely designed by Him.

Jesus, God's only begotten Son.
Jesus He is the Heavenly and Holy One.
Jesus born of a virgin and came to be.
Jesus "I love you," God said to His Son and to me.
Jesus gave us a new commandment in how we are to live.
Jesus said we are, "to love one another as I have loved you."

Love was created in His own image.
Love and care God has truly shown.
Love like this no man has ever known.
Love a life born for you and me.
Love a life taken at Calvary.

Love He wipes away our tears.
Love we no longer have to fear.
Love grace and mercy are shown.
Love an essential part of my day.
Love He allows me to find a better way.

"For God so loved the world..." John 3:16 says.
Jesus was born and this day we celebrate His birth.
A prophecy fulfilled.
It comes with a great Christmas message of, "I LOVE YOU!"

"This is My commandment, that you love one another as I have loved you." John 15:12 (NKJV)

Jesus: The Joy of Christmas

What a blissful Christmas season that lies ahead.
I can hear and sense the presence of joy in the air.
For we are blessed and it is because of You,
Our Lord and Savior Jesus Christ.
You are the Anointed One.

We are grateful for Christmas and what it means.
The Messiah, our King is born.
He has come to give us life more abundantly.
Jesus it is You who sets the captive free.
Our Wonderful Counselor and Prince of Peace is He.

Adonai we say "Hallelujah" to You.
My Lord it is You who reigns.
Adoration, glory, and splendor it all belongs to you.
Thank you, Jesus, for all that you do.

Blessed and highly favored are we.
For you have given your people great victory.
At the right hand of God our Heavenly Father You sit.
Your unfailing and endless love never quits.

Oh Lion of Judah how we await your return.
We lift our hands in honor of You.
Your presence, Your love, so sweet and tender too.
Behold the Lamb of God this Christmas day.
As we go and prepare ye the way.

"Hallelujah to the Lord" is our praise.
Glory to God in the highest our voices raise.
Emmanuel, God with us.
We behold You and celebrate the joy of Christmas.

"...they saw the young Child with Mary His mother, and fell down and worshiped Him." Matthew 2:11 (NKJV)

Jesus, the Messiah
Happy Birthday to You!

God in His awesomeness this day came to be.
He thought of you and He thought of me.
A time of celebration.
A time of victory.
Oh what a wonderful Christmas this will be.
As I look to Emmanuel and see…
My Lord, My Savior, and me.

I rejoice as I reflect on what this season truly means.
It gives me eternal life, a day of love, sprinkled with peace.
As the time draws nearer it is Jesus that I seek.
A babe in a manger, the Messiah is He.
All wrapped into one God the Father created
   and called the Lord to be.
The One who came to set the captive free.
My Lord, My Savior, just for you and me.

When I look and see what is to come,
humbled I am because You thought of me.
I lift my hands surrendering all to You.
Grateful for a love wonderful and true.
For I've learned, it's not about me.
But it's all about You.
My Lord, My Savior, Jesus it is You!

Christmas time - a season full of song and cheer.
Praises of adoration flow with loved ones so near.
As we recognize and acknowledge You are here.
The blessings of the Lord they do shine through.
Grateful for this time as we draw closer and say to you.
"Jesus, the Messiah, Happy Birthday to You!"

"Let everything that has breath praise the LORD." Psalm 150:6 (NKJV)

Oh! What a Year

Oh what a year of blessings we've seen.
Oh what a year of hope that gleams.
Oh what a year of memories to cherish.
Oh what a year to live and not perish.

This season so sweet only God could design.
A season of joy and great peace of mind.
Trusting in Him and learning each day.
You have a life to live that never fades away.

Smiles on faces – all the girls and boys.
With hearts that leap with such great joy.
No reason to be sad or frown today.
The love of Jesus is here to stay.

Christmas is here.
Jesus' season of love.
A gift sent from heaven.
From our Father up above.

So take a moment to stop and reflect,
On the blessings you have – with no neglect.
As a New Year is just ahead.
Talk with the Father to be led.

See what's new that's coming your way.
No one knows, but God does say,
Take no thought for tomorrow you see,
For He knows just what it will be.
Keep your eyes focused on me.
Oh what a year we all will see.

"…He is Lord of all." Acts 10:36 (NKJV)

The Adoration of a Great King

The adoration of a great King.
A song of praise and worship is what I bring.
Bowing down before You - the Holy One.
You are God's only begotten Son.

A precious baby born in a manger.
This was You Jesus not a stranger.
Your birth is such a miracle in itself.
Greater than any man's power or wealth.

I adore you O Holy One.
Rejoicing with the angels I do sing.
Glory be to the newborn King.
"Alleluia, Alleluia" let the myriad of praises ring.

Your life came forth to save a world.
Not just a man or woman, but every boy and girl.
Scriptures were written telling us what to do.
Praise the Lord! Praise ye the Lord!
Grace, blessings, and adoration all belongs to You.

Jesus I honor You with great reverence.
I give glory and admiration to You.
With my heart filled this wonderful Christmas Day.
I acknowledge You Lord in an extraordinary way.

Exaltation it all belongs to You.
So thank You Jesus for a love so true.
I lift my hands to You in surrender.
In glorification and with awesome splendor.

You are celebrated in such a joyful and glorious way.
For You my Lord were born on Christmas Day.
No one else could transcend into life like You.
Jesus You are so faithful and true.

Adoration I have for such a great King.
This is the song that my heart sings.
Looking for You to come again.
My Savior, my Lord, and my best Friend.

"Oh, magnify the Lord with me, and let us exalt His name together."
Psalm 34:3 (NKJV)

The Best Gift for This Season

Celebration time is nearing.
For the Christmas season is ringing in.
People are starting to scurry all across the land.
But do they really and truly understand?

As the commotion goes along,
do they know why they are here?
The people run to gather their gifts and games.
But do they know why Jesus came?

Parents try to fulfill what the children's wishes are.
Do they know what Christ wish is for them?
Eternity was the best gift that could be offered,
for each and every one of us.
The Father fulfilled a prophecy, a promise that He made.

So, no list do you have to make.
No scurrying necessary and crowds do you have to take.
God's gift is eternal.
Jesus came that we might be free and have eternity.
Feel in your heart the love of Christ and what His birth means.

Seek Him while he may be sought.
Reach Him and learn all that is to be taught.
God is good and we want all that is available.
Remember and realize that He is able.

Search your heart and find the one sent from above.
Come and experience His love.
Receive it today.
And don't let this opportunity slip away.
As you shop for a present or two,
  remember the gift God gave you!

"For God so loved the world that He gave His only begotten Son, that whoever believes in Him should not perish but have everlasting life."
John 3:16 (NJKV)

The Gift of Life

As I look down the road, there is a figure I see. It is my Heavenly Father coming to greet me. Oh my child, what do you need? I'm not sure Dad. Nothing in particular for me.

"There is something you need to know. Life was given for you. So you can live. So you can grow. Affectionately, I thought of you. A life you will live full of grace and love too."

A walk with Me one gets to take. It is the gift of life. It's nothing one could fake. Grab a hold of it and embrace it too. This gift of life was created for you.

Confession is all one has to make. Embrace it now and a step you take. God's Son created just for me. The gift of life, He did breathe. A price paid, yes, in full. No gift too small from God any day. Thanks for Jesus. The Gift of Life has shown us the way.

His presence felt in all you do.
The love of the Father wonderful and true.
A new day for you.
A new year approaching too.

Enjoy this Christmas season and
  the splendor that it brings.
Hallelujah to the New Born King!

"For unto us a Child is born, Unto us a Son is given;...And His name will be called Wonderful, Counselor, Mighty God, Everlasting Father, Prince of Peace." (Isaiah 9:6) (NKJV)

The Many Blessings of the Lord

As I approach a New Year, I reflect on many things…
The beauty of this life I have seen.
The love of God that I have felt.
The peace that dwells within me.
I know in my heart, I have seen the many blessings of the Lord.

Holidays come and holidays may go.
One thing I do know for sure.
I have seen the many blessings of the Lord.

With my family and friends the Lord has given me.
I take them not for granted, because I know they are a gift from thee.

So with all these blessings my Father has given,
I look and smile for each day is new to me.
Lord, keep your presence ever so near.
We need to continue this walk into a New Year.
For I know there are many more blessings ahead.

This season of joy, love, and peace.
Granted by God, who is My Heavenly Father.
Jesus is His Son who came for you and me.
As we go forward to enjoy another year,
I realize new blessings are oh so near.

Lord, please take our hand as we go through
To enjoy the love that flows from you.
The time has come for us to grow near,
To you Father God and to have no fears.
For this coming year we've got new blessings to see.

Jesus is Lord for you and for me.
Let's remember as we reflect upon our past.
God's continued love and our faith will last.
Journeys never end and neither does the race.
Till we see you Lord, face-to-face.

"…I have come that they may have life, and that they may have it more abundantly." John 10:10 (NKJV)

This Christmas Season

The bells begin to ring.
The Christmas carolers come out and sing.
Fresh, crisp air to take in.
Oh, let the Christmas season begin.

A year of joy, filled with laughter.
Some days of turmoil would fall in after.
Overall, we're blessed you see.
A new Christmas season for you and me.

The love of the Father so rich and true.
Sent us His blessed Son Jesus to see us through.
Grace, love, and mercy bestowed today.
As we recognize the love of Jesus this holiday.

As we reach forth to a new year ahead.
Many blessings flow from above unto where we are led.
Joy lies ahead on this path you see.
Stop and take in the smell from the fresh pine trees.

A holiday season unique in its own way.
Seek out your many blessings today.
Enjoy this time with family and friends.
Take in this season that has no end.

Jesus is Lord in this relationship so true.
Do you know how much He really loves you?
Call Him today as you approach a new year.
Seek out the Lord and have no fear.

Tributes of Love

The love of God is so real. Love captivates the heart and flows from God to man. I acknowledge the love of Jesus. It is so strong and powerful that it can overwhelm anything or anyone, if you allow it to. This love doesn't end with Christmas. It lives on throughout the year. I have found some very special women that exhibit the love of God.

I say to God thank you. To Jesus thank you. And to the Holy Spirit thank you.

In finalizing the Christmas messages, there are some tributes that I have written. The love felt and experienced from these individuals come from God. It shows me love that truly flows from the heart. These tributes I want to share with you. Only God can create this kind of person who demonstrates the true meaning of a devout and nurturing woman. She is God's creation.

A Mother's Love

The amazing person you are is so dear to me.
The love you give is constant and free.
It flows no matter what I do.
One thing I know for sure is Mother, I love you!

Your kindness and compassion to so many you show.
It lets everyone know who you are.
I'm so glad to say you are my Mom.
When it comes down to it, I'd rather you.

Day in and day out, I learn from you.
The daily challenges are erased when your smile shines through.
She is a precious gift of beauty, radiant and true.
My Mom a special gem that is a testament God to you.

I walk this life filled with precious memories of the things we do.
You watched me take my first step.
You dealt with all of my changes from adolescence to adulthood.
I thank God for a Mom like you.

I couldn't have imagined growing up to be like you.
Those precious gems now shine in me too.
A mantle of love from my mother I wear today.
For a double portion is what I pray.

No one could ever fill your shoes.
God designed your personality to fit only you.
The uniqueness He created was fashioned just for you.
The fine qualities only a mother could display.
So this Lord is what I pray.

Thank you Lord for a mother kind and true.
Living out the love of Jesus as it shines through.
No one else could form us in our mother's womb.
It took our Heavenly Father to create and bless you.
I love you Mother.

A Woman Named Lucretia Bee

Some people in life play an important role.
Not knowing in the beginning how they would bless your soul.
I can say Lucretia Bee did that for me.
More than a Grandmother she came to be.

Stature – so strong and tall.
"Hey Boo" as you were called.
A laugh no one could replicate.
Now she stands at the Pearly Gates.

Our Heavenly Father she is with now.
The chance at Jesus' feet to bow.
One day she heard that great call.
In this life, she gave her all.

No more pain her body to take.
It was all so real – this life no joke, not fake.
Rest in God's love, we all must do.
A requirement for me and you.

Another soldier crossed over the other day.
A new address and she's on her way.
God knows the life that was shared.
Deep down inside Miss Lucretia truly cared.

Love she gave to her family.
A priceless gift; such a great legacy.
A woman in her seasoned years.
Challenges handled with less fears.

Grandma, you will be missed.
All I have are the memories and a kiss.
"Trust in the Lord," you would always say.
We have to because Jesus is the only way!

"Trust in the LORD with all your heart, and lean not on your own understanding; in all your ways acknowledge Him, and He shall direct your paths." Proverbs 3:5-6 (NKJV)

A Woman of Strength and Honor

A woman of strength and honor is she.
No matter the trial she has to face.
She remains strong and holds to her faith
God at the head of her life, with her every step of the way.
Clinging to the Word and what it has to say.

A wife and mother roles she wears like a cloak.
This destiny she has been charged with and holds to her heart.
So important to her with great dedication she carries.
A virtuous woman, no less she has been.
She offers love to everyone, family or friend.
She rises early for her family, to meet every need.
Making sure we were prepared for the day.

As grandmother and great-grandmother her legacy extends.
Her name lives on in two of them.
So much love in her entire family that it fills her life.
Many children were cared for and loved in her home.
She has been a friend to many who have come along.
No one cast out, but received with love.

This woman, an ambassador for Christ, who has shared the Word.
Be it a Sunday school teacher, a missionary, or in her daily walk of life
She surrendered and served God in every capacity.
She did the best she could as the obstacles of life she faced.
Never forsaken by God for He gave His amazing grace.
"My God, my God, You have always been there."

A treasure of love to me my Mom has been.
A wealth of knowledge and kindness she shared.
A woman of strength, honor, faith, and courage.
That is who my Mom is.

At the end of her journey, at the Pearly Gates she stands.
To be greeted by Jesus with His arms open wide.
"I made it Lord, this life I survived!"
All the pain erased and tears washed away.
I'm seeing my Lord and Savior face-to-face today.
Remember the good times, until we meet again.

Mother I Love You Even Today

Mother I love you even today.
These words I must say.
It is because of your loving kindness.
You shared this with me everyday.

I looked for your smile that brightens my day.
I listened for your soft voice that says everything is okay.
The way you greeted me when I come through the door.
So much love - I couldn't ask for anything more.

Mother I love you.
From the bottom of my heart, I really do.
My heart grateful and blessed to be given to you.
So I thank you Lord for all my mother could do.

A mother's love no one can replicate.
A special recipe God created and it lives within.
Thank you Mom for the compassion that flowed from you.
You were so special to me and our family too.

A wonderful treasure and a priceless gem.
You were filled with love, faith, hope, and joy.
Those pearls of wisdom I didn't always get.
I was not sure at first, but now I understand your keen wit.

So here I stand a beautiful reflection of you I see.
Those fine qualities have become a part of me.
You mastered the gift of what a mother should be.
Mother your wonderful love lives in me.

Thank you for the virtuous woman you were.
Thank you for the special love that you gave.
Thank you for the prayers that you prayed.
Thank you for teaching me Jesus is the way.

Please know this," Mother I love you even today!"

Woman...This is You

Woman...this is you.
Mothers, sisters, daughters, and friends.
Beautiful they are formed.
Built as nurturers, so full of love.
Uniquely designed in your own way.
Strong, confident, this is you.

Woman...
Matriarchs in your own right.
Destined to survive.
Legacy created through this family tree.
Life given to solidify history.
Faithful and dedicated; this is you.

Woman...
Trusting in heart.
Desiring to be a friend.
More than that, memories you make, they won't end.
Children at your knee – full of life and glee.

Woman...
My mother, my sister, my daughter, and my friend.
Realize life flows from you.
Teach us all you can
Understanding we must be true.

Woman...this is you.
Laughter - today and tomorrow.
Even when my heart is full of sorrow.
United in faith: in bond with me.

I honor you and treasure who you are today.
No one can steal or take your joy away.
Empowered to stand.
A mission to complete.

Woman...she is whole.
Not easy to defeat.
Your beauty, your essence.
The crown that you wear
People calling out, echoing your name.

Woman…this is your day!
A great gift from God we are.
He is near – never too far.
Woman… a treasure from God.

You Are An Awesome Mom

You are an awesome Mom and you wear this title well.
It truly attests to the woman that you are.
A nurturer, full of love, kindness, and God's abundant grace.
I listen for your voice, o God, and it makes my day.
It is the care and love that you so freely give.
For you teach us that is how to love and live.

Your smile brightens my day.
The kisses and hugs mean so much to me.
I thank God for blessing me with you.
You are one of His virtuous women and that light shines through.

We do praise you for what you do.
You show us how to love and treat others too.
"Train up a child," this is what you've taught me.
I haven't strayed from the path called victory.
Obediently and unselfishly I follow your steps.

The sacrifices you make.
You don't even complain.
To hear the happiness in your children's voice.
That is all you need – so simple and plain.

A treasure of riches you have been.
My Mother, nurturer, confidant, and a great friend.
I finally see and understand all you have done.
So now I'm on this path and follow your lead.

I know at the end satisfaction is there.
A sense of accomplish.
Filled with great love and care.
So an awesome Mom this is what you do.

You are truly a precious and priceless gem.
Yes, many call her blessed and praise her too.
I'm grateful for this path Jesus has led me on.
More than a virtuous woman, that is who you are.
An awesome Mom who stands confident and strong.

*Give her of the fruit of her hands, And let her own works praise
her in the gates. (Proverbs 31:31) (NKJV)*

About the Author

Natalie Selena Bee enjoys writing poetry. It has become a passion of hers for many years. "Each piece always has something new to reflect upon and ultimately share with others. The Christmas messages do come from my heart." Making sure she has a message written each October is so important to her. Natalie gets to acknowledge Jesus and His birth. Such a priceless gift to behold. Such an honor to utilize the gifts and talents she has been blessed with.

Words of comfort, inspiration, and strength flow as she writes about life and the goodness of God. She has published two books of inspirational poetry entitled, "Defining Moments in Life: Poetic Expressions" and "Reflections of the Inner Spirit: Poetic Inspirations". She has written a Christmas message for over 20 years and shares with the masses. She has shared her poetic inspirations on a recent mission trip to Managua, Nicaragua.

Natalie accepted Jesus Christ as her Lord and Savior at a young age. It is a firm foundation that her life continues to be built upon. For many years, she has served in numerous areas of ministry. Being a servant of God takes priority in her life. She is a member of Abundant Life Church.

Natalie is a graduate of Coker College with a Bachelor's Degree in Business Administration. She has received a diploma from Rhema Correspondence Bible School.

(back cover)

www.ingramcontent.com/pod-product-compliance
Lightning Source LLC
La Vergne TN
LVHW041210080426
835508LV00008B/882